Growth Breaks Us Through Our Own Outer Layer to Flourish With Aliveness.

Feed Your Fire: Provisions for Fulfillment™

Copyright ©2023 by Picasso Foods

First Edition

All rights reserved. Printed in the United States of America. No part of this book may be used or reproduced in any matter whatsoever without written permission except in the case of brief quotations embodied in critical articles and reviews.

For more information, visit:
www.prochiplantenergy.com.

Feed Your
FIRE

This journal and guidebook will take you on a journey of discovery with thoughtful prompts and provocations interspersed with levity, creativity, and of course - food.

Lentils, our star ingredient, are as much a metaphor as they are a source of nourishment. They are the seeds that give way to bloom, representing the circle of life and good fortune.

What Does Fulfillment Mean to You?

_____

_____

_____

_____

_____

_____

_____

_____

_____

_____

THE GREATEST ADVENTURE IS TO **EXPLORE WHO YOU ARE.**

– Unknown

If you strip away age, gender, occupation, and the roles you play in life, what do you see? What are your core beliefs? Rather than reflecting on what you are, consider who you are. Put it into words.

_____

_____

_____

_____

_____

_____

_____

_____

_____

_____

_____

_____

_____

_____

_____

_____

Your Authentic Self

*Be Still
In Your Heart
and
Keep Moving.*

FOREVER IS COMPOSED OF NOWS.

– Emily Dickinson

Are you focused on the present or pulling from the past? Move beyond memories and step into what's happening now. Take time to reflect on what's in front of you without fear of what's next. What is good about the present moment? What does it tell you? What does it offer you?

_____

_____

_____

_____

_____

_____

_____

_____

_____

_____

_____

_____

_____

_____

The Present Moment

Coconut Lentils

Coconut Lentils

Ingredients

3 T. olive oil
1 small onion, small diced
3 cloves garlic, minced
1" peeled fresh ginger, finely chopped
1 t . jalapeño, seeded and finely chopped (optional)
2 3/4 C. water
1 lb. red lentils
1 can of coconut milk
1 t. salt
Juice of 1 lime
1/4 C. cilantro, chopped

Heat oil in a large saucepan over medium heat. Add onion and sauté about 5 minutes until translucent. Add garlic, ginger and jalapeño and cook for about 30 seconds. Add water. Rinse and drain lentils and add to pot. Reserve 1/2 C. coconut milk, and add remaining milk from can to pot. Bring to a boil. Then, reduce heat to simmer and let cook for 8-10 minutes. Add salt, lime juice, cilantro, and reserved coconut milk and stir. Let cook an additional 2-5 minutes. The lentils should be tender but not mushy. Serve warm.

Bonus: top with fried onions or shallots.

Vegan | Gluten Free

Serves 6.

FOR THE LOVE OF LENTILS

YOU WILL FIND THAT IT IS NECESSARY TO LET THINGS GO; SIMPLY FOR THE REASON THAT THEY ARE HEAVY. SO LET THEM GO, LET GO OF THEM. I TIE NO WEIGHTS TO MY ANKLES.

- C. JoyBell C.

Are you holding onto something that you need to release? Something you loved and lost? A belief set that no longer serves you? A resentment or regret? Identify it and then imagine it dissolving in your fingertips. Speak to it and yourself with compassion, as you set it down and acknowledge what you feel in that moment.

_____

_____

_____

_____

_____

_____

_____

_____

_____

_____

_____

_____

_____

_____

_____

_____

Release What Holds You Back

Guide Yourself with the Question, "Who Do I Want to Become?"

THE ONLY THING WORSE THAN HAVING NO SIGHT IS HAVING NO VISION.

– Helen Keller

Close your eyes and imagine your life 15 years from now. What do you see? What do you look like? Where are you living? How are you spending your time? How does it feel? Now work your way backwards doing the same exercise for 10 years from now and then five years. With a clear vision, you can set out with intention.

_____

_____

_____

_____

_____

_____

_____

_____

_____

_____

_____

_____

_____

_____

_____

_____

Envisioning

WHATEVER WE **BELIEVE ABOUT OURSELVES** AND OUR ABILITY COMES TRUE FOR US.

- Susan L. Taylor

What do you know to be true for yourself? If there was no one to please, get validation from, or influence your beliefs, what would you see inside of you? How can you work toward truly honoring all that you are and have to offer?

_____

_____

_____

_____

_____

_____

_____

_____

_____

_____

_____

_____

_____

_____

_____

_____

Valuing Yourself

Reacting Perpetuates the Past.

Responding Creates a New Future.

EVERYTHING YOU WANT IS ON THE OTHER SIDE OF FEAR.

- Jack Canfield

We can convince ourselves that there is an external obstacle, when it is our fear holding us back. Seeing this truth requires releasing expectations and shame. What would happen if you embraced something new? What would happen if you allowed yourself to rise? How could you grow regardless of the outcome?

_____

_____

_____

_____

_____

_____

_____

_____

_____

_____

_____

_____

_____

_____

Pushing Past Fear

Classic Lentil Soup

Classic Lentil Soup

Ingredients
3 T. olive oil
1 small onion, small diced
2 carrots, small diced
1 celery stalk, small diced
2 cloves garlic, minced
1/4 t. red pepper flakes
1 lb. french green or puy lentils, rinsed and drained
8 C. chicken or vegetable stock
1 C. tomato sauce
3 bay leaves
Leaves from 4 sprigs of thyme (optional but preferred)
1/2 t. salt
Pepper
2 T. chopped parsley
1/4 C. Parmesan cheese, grated

Heat oil in a large saucepan over medium heat. Add onion, carrots, and celery and sauté about 5 minutes until onions are translucent and vegetables are slightly tender. Add garlic and red pepper flakes and cook for about 30 seconds. Add lentils, stock and tomato sauce. Add bay leaves and thyme. Bring to a boil. Then, reduce heat to simmer and let cook for 15-20 minutes. Season with salt and pepper. The lentils should be tender but not mushy. Remove from heat and add parsley. Remove bay leaves before serving and top each bowl with a spoonful of Parmesan cheese.

Vegan | Gluten Free

Serves 6.

FOR THE LOVE OF LENTILS

CHANGE IS HARD AT FIRST, MESSY IN THE MIDDLE, AND GORGEOUS AT THE END.

– Robin Sharma

When we change ourselves, we change our circumstances. Reflect on things that have changed for the better. What was the catalyst? What could you control in those moments and what did you have to accept?

_____

_____

_____

_____

_____

_____

_____

_____

_____

_____

_____

_____

_____

_____

_____

_____

_____

Transformation

Illuminate the World. It Needs Your Light.

THE MEANING OF LIFE IS TO FIND YOUR GIFT.

THE PURPOSE OF LIFE IS TO GIVE IT AWAY.

– Pablo Picasso

Take a moment to acknowledge your gifts and talents, personality, and experiences. What do they say about you? How can you use them to interact with the world around you? How could others benefit from your perspective?

_____

_____

_____

_____

_____

_____

_____

_____

_____

_____

_____

_____

_____

_____

_____

_____

Living with Intention

A Favorite Lentil Salad... Multiple Options.

A Favorite Lentil Salad

Ingredients
1 lb. black lentils, rinsed and drained
6 C. water
3 bay leaves
Salt and pepper

Dressing
1 T. shallot, minced
1 1/2 t. ground mustard
1 T. maple syrup
3 T. champagne vinegar
8 T. avocado oil
Salt and pepper

Toppings (Option 1)
One avocado, diced
1 C. grape tomatoes, quartered
3 green onions
Garnish with chopped cilantro

Toppings (Option 2)
1 C. grapes, sliced
1/3. C. walnuts
Garnish with chopped parsley

In a large saucepan, combine lentils, water and bay leaves. Bring to a boil and then reduce to simmer. Let cook about 10-15 minutes or until tender. Drain and remove bay leaves. Season with salt and pepper.

In a small bowl, whisk together shallot, mustard, maple syrup, and champagne vinegar. Add in avocado oil slowly, whisking constantly. Season with salt and pepper.

Combine lentils with dressing. Add toppings. Taste. Season with salt and pepper, as needed. Serve warm or cold.

Vegan | Gluten Free

Serves 6.

FOOD IS SYMBOLIC OF LOVE WHEN WORDS ARE INADEQUATE.

- Alan D. Wolfelt

Food is not just a functional experience, it is an emotional one. What is your relationship with food? What do you believe food represents? How can it facilitate your love for yourself and connection to others?

_____

_____

_____

_____

_____

_____

_____

_____

_____

_____

_____

_____

_____

_____

_____

Your Relationship with Food

A Work in Progress is a Beautiful Thing.

GRACE IS THE FACE THAT LOVE WEARS WHEN IT MEETS IMPERFECTION.

– Joseph R. Cooke

Are you offering yourself compassion when faced with a challenge? Have you put unreasonable expectations on yourself or others? Consider mistakes, difficulties, or losses that weigh on your mind and how you could more lovingly relate to them.

_____

_____

_____

_____

_____

_____

_____

_____

_____

_____

_____

_____

_____

_____

_____

_____

_____

_____

Releasing Expectation

LOVE AND COMPASSION ARE NECESSITIES, NOT LUXURIES. WITHOUT THEM, HUMANITY CANNOT SURVIVE.

– Dalai Lama

How do you define the human experience? Consider your views on connecting with others and how that could become more expansive.

_____

_____

_____

_____

_____

_____

_____

_____

_____

_____

_____

_____

_____

_____

_____

_____

Expansion

Choose in Creation of Your Best Life and a Better World.

FUN IS ONE OF THE MOST IMPORTANT – AND UNDERRATED – INGREDIENTS...

- Richard Branson

What invigorates you or makes you laugh? Do those things! You have one life to live so find the joy no matter the circumstance. Those are the moments you will remember and that will fuel your tomorrow. Fun can be quiet enjoyment, it can be intimate, it can be bold. What would you like to explore? How can you find the fun in what you already do?

_____

_____

_____

_____

_____

_____

_____

_____

_____

_____

_____

_____

_____

_____

Pursue Delight

HAPPINESS IS LETTING GO OF WHAT YOU THINK YOUR LIFE IS SUPPOSED TO LOOK LIKE, AND CELEBRATING IT FOR EVERYTHING THAT IT IS.

– Mandy Hale

Expectations create a false narrative that's written in your mind. Throw them away and celebrate your unique journey and what you have overcome. How have you prevailed? How have you grown? How have you loved? Rewrite your life story with this mindset.

_____

_____

_____

_____

_____

_____

_____

_____

_____

_____

_____

_____

_____

_____

_____

_____

Rewrite Your Narrative

Some Things Just Are & that's Okay.

There is Beauty in the Seasons.

CHANGE YOUR THOUGHTS, AND YOU CHANGE YOUR WORLD.

– Norman Vincent Peale

There is science behind the idea that our thoughts create our reality. Changing your thoughts requires becoming aware of your natural patterns and practicing new ideas and perspective. Can you challenge your mindset and think differently about something in your life? Write this down and practice it daily. Take notice of the changes you experience.

_____

_____

_____

_____

_____

_____

_____

_____

_____

_____

_____

_____

_____

_____

_____

Rethinking

What Would Happen if You Reached for the Unknown?

Inside cabbage looks remarkably like a flower.
What do you see when you get curious?

www.ingramcontent.com/pod-product-compliance
Lightning Source LLC
Chambersburg PA
CBHW051601010526
44118CB00023B/2776